THIS JOURNAL BEL⟨

D1365657

_____

_____

_____

*Please return if found and respect my privacy by
not reading any further. Thank you!*

SEASONS FALL PRAYER JOURNAL - BLACK & WHITE EDITION

All Bible verses from the English Standard Version (ESV)

Printed in the United States of America

ISBN: 9781689048866

www.HolyJustLove.com

CALENDAR

MONTH

YEAR

CALENDAR

SUN	MON	TUE	WED	THU	FRI	SAT
OFFERING:						
OFFERING:						
OFFERING:						
OFFERING:						
OFFERING:						

The plans of the diligent lead surely to abundance,
but everyone who is hasty comes only to poverty. ~ Psalm 37:4-5

SUNDAY

MONDAY

TUESDAY

WEDNESDAY

THURSDAY

FRIDAY

SATURDAY

WEEKLY GOALS

WEEK OF

PRIORITIES

WEEKLY GOALS

WEEK OF

SUNDAY

MONDAY

TUESDAY

WEDNESDAY

THURSDAY

FRIDAY

SATURDAY

PRIORITIES

SUNDAY

MONDAY

TUESDAY

WEDNESDAY

THURSDAY

FRIDAY

SATURDAY

WEEKLY GOALS

WEEK OF

PRIORITIES

WEEKLY GOALS

WEEK OF

SUNDAY

MONDAY

TUESDAY

WEDNESDAY

THURSDAY

FRIDAY

SATURDAY

PRIORITIES

SUNDAY

MONDAY

TUESDAY

WEDNESDAY

THURSDAY

FRIDAY

SATURDAY

WEEKLY GOALS

WEEK OF

PRIORITIES

MONTH

YEAR

CALENDAR

SUN	MON	TUE	WED	THU	FRI	SAT
OFFERING:						
OFFERING:						
OFFERING:						
OFFERING:						
OFFERING:						

But you, take courage! Do not let your hands be weak, for your work shall be rewarded."
Proverbs 21:5

SUNDAY

MONDAY

TUESDAY

WEDNESDAY

THURSDAY

FRIDAY

SATURDAY

WEEKLY GOALS

WEEK OF

PRIORITIES

WEEKLY GOALS

WEEK OF

PRIORITIES

SUNDAY

MONDAY

TUESDAY

WEDNESDAY

THURSDAY

FRIDAY

SATURDAY

SUNDAY

MONDAY

TUESDAY

WEDNESDAY

THURSDAY

FRIDAY

SATURDAY

WEEKLY GOALS

WEEK OF

PRIORITIES

SUNDAY

MONDAY

TUESDAY

WEDNESDAY

THURSDAY

FRIDAY

SATURDAY

WEEKLY GOALS

WEEK OF

PRIORITIES

SUNDAY

MONDAY

TUESDAY

WEDNESDAY

THURSDAY

FRIDAY

SATURDAY

WEEKLY GOALS

WEEK OF

PRIORITIES

MONTH

YEAR

CALENDAR

SUN	MON	TUE	WED	THU	FRI	SAT
OFFERING:						
OFFERING:						
OFFERING:						
OFFERING:						
OFFERING:						

The heart of man plans his way, but the Lord establishes his steps.
Proverbs 16:19

SUNDAY

MONDAY

TUESDAY

WEDNESDAY

THURSDAY

FRIDAY

SATURDAY

WEEKLY GOALS

WEEK OF

PRIORITIES

WEEKLY GOALS

WEEK OF

SUNDAY

MONDAY

TUESDAY

WEDNESDAY

PRIORITIES

THURSDAY

FRIDAY

SATURDAY

SUNDAY

MONDAY

TUESDAY

WEDNESDAY

THURSDAY

FRIDAY

SATURDAY

WEEKLY GOALS

WEEK OF

PRIORITIES

SUNDAY

MONDAY

TUESDAY

WEDNESDAY

THURSDAY

FRIDAY

SATURDAY

WEEKLY GOALS

WEEK OF

PRIORITIES

SUNDAY

MONDAY

TUESDAY

WEDNESDAY

THURSDAY

FRIDAY

SATURDAY

WEEKLY GOALS

WEEK OF

PRIORITIES

MONTH

YEAR

CALENDAR

SUN	MON	TUE	WED	THU	FRI	SAT
OFFERING:						
OFFERING:						
OFFERING:						
OFFERING:						
OFFERING:						

Trust in the LORD with all your heart And do not lean on your own understanding. In all your ways acknowledge Him, And He will make your paths straight. ~ Proverbs 3:5-6

SUNDAY

MONDAY

TUESDAY

WEDNESDAY

THURSDAY

FRIDAY

SATURDAY

WEEKLY GOALS

WEEK OF

PRIORITIES

SUNDAY

WEEKLY GOALS
WEEK OF

MONDAY

PRIORITIES

TUESDAY

WEDNESDAY

THURSDAY

FRIDAY

SATURDAY

SUNDAY

MONDAY

TUESDAY

WEDNESDAY

THURSDAY

FRIDAY

SATURDAY

WEEKLY GOALS

WEEK OF

PRIORITIES

SUNDAY

MONDAY

TUESDAY

WEDNESDAY

THURSDAY

FRIDAY

SATURDAY

WEEKLY GOALS

WEEK OF

PRIORITIES

SUNDAY

MONDAY

TUESDAY

WEDNESDAY

THURSDAY

FRIDAY

SATURDAY

WEEKLY GOALS

WEEK OF

PRIORITIES

JOURNAL

AREAS FOR DESIRED GROWTH FOR THIS SEASON:

Date

Rejoice always, pray without ceasing, give thanks in all circumstances;
for this is the will of God in Christ Jesus for you. ~ 1 Thessalonians 5:16-18

DAILY BIBLE VERSE

ADORATION

CONFESSION

THANKSGIVING

SUPPLICATION

DAILY PRAYER JOURNAL

And this is the confidence that we have toward him, that if we ask anything according to his will he hears us. ~ 1 John 5:14

DAILY BIBLE VERSE

ADORATION

CONFESSION

THANKSGIVING

SUPPLICATION

Date

Do not be anxious about anything, but in everything by prayer and supplication with thanksgiving let your requests be made known to God. ~ Philippians 4:6

DAILY BIBLE VERSE

ADORATION

CONFESSION

THANKSGIVING

SUPPLICATION

DAILY PRAYER JOURNAL

Continue steadfastly in prayer, being watchful in it with thanksgiving.
~ Colossians 4:2

DAILY BIBLE VERSE

ADORATION

CONFESSION

THANKSGIVING

SUPPLICATION

DAILY PRAYER JOURNAL

Date

Therefore I tell you, whatever you ask in prayer, believe that you have received it, and it will be yours. ~ Mark 11:24

DAILY BIBLE VERSE

ADORATION

CONFESSION

THANKSGIVING

SUPPLICATION

DAILY PRAYER JOURNAL

Then you will call upon me and come and pray to me, and I will hear you.
~ Jeremiah 29:12

DAILY BIBLE VERSE

ADORATION

CONFESSION

THANKSGIVING

SUPPLICATION

Date

Rejoice in hope, be patient in tribulation, be constant in prayer.
~ Romans 12:12

DAILY BIBLE VERSE

ADORATION

CONFESSION

THANKSGIVING

SUPPLICATION

DAILY PRAYER JOURNAL

The Lord is near to all who call on him, to all who call on him in truth.
~ Psalm 145:18

DAILY BIBLE VERSE

ADORATION

CONFESSION

THANKSGIVING

SUPPLICATION

DAILY PRAYER JOURNAL

For where two or three are gathered in my name, there am I among them.
~ Matthew 18:20

DAILY BIBLE VERSE

ADORATION

CONFESSION

THANKSGIVING

SUPPLICATION

Let us then with confidence draw near to the throne of grace, that we may receive mercy and find grace to help in time of need. ~ Hebrews 4:16

DAILY BIBLE VERSE

ADORATION

CONFESSION

THANKSGIVING

SUPPLICATION

DAILY PRAYER JOURNAL

But when you pray, go into your room and shut the door and pray to your Father who is in secret. And your Father who sees in secret will reward you. ~ Matthew 6:6

DAILY BIBLE VERSE

ADORATION

CONFESSION

THANKSGIVING

SUPPLICATION

In my distress I called upon the Lord; to my God I cried for help. From his temple he heard my voice, and my cry to him reached his ears. ~ Psalm 18:6

DAILY BIBLE VERSE

ADORATION

CONFESSION

THANKSGIVING

SUPPLICATION

Date

And if we know that he hears us in whatever we ask, we know that we have the requests that we have asked of him. ~ 1 John 5:15

DAILY BIBLE VERSE

ADORATION

CONFESSION

THANKSGIVING

SUPPLICATION

DAILY PRAYER JOURNAL

Therefore, confess your sins to one another and pray for one another, that you may be healed. The prayer of a righteous person has great power as it is working. ~ James 5:16

DAILY BIBLE VERSE

ADORATION

CONFESSION

THANKSGIVING

SUPPLICATION

DAILY PRAYER JOURNAL

But let him ask in faith, with no doubting, for the one who doubts is like a wave of the sea that is driven and tossed by the wind. ~ James 1:6

DAILY BIBLE VERSE

ADORATION

CONFESSION

THANKSGIVING

SUPPLICATION

bless those who curse you, pray for those who abuse you. ~ Luke 6:28

DAILY BIBLE VERSE

ADORATION

CONFESSION

THANKSGIVING

SUPPLICATION

DAILY PRAYER JOURNAL

Date

DAILY PRAYER JOURNAL

The end of all things is at hand; therefore be self-controlled and sober-minded for the sake of your prayers. ~ 1 Peter 4:7

DAILY BIBLE VERSE

ADORATION

CONFESSION

THANKSGIVING

SUPPLICATION

...For we do not know what to pray for as we ought, but the Spirit himself intercedes for us with groanings too deep for words. ~ Romans 8:26b

DAILY BIBLE VERSE

ADORATION

CONFESSION

THANKSGIVING

SUPPLICATION

Date

O Lord, in the morning you hear my voice;
in the morning I prepare a sacrifice for you and watch. ~ Psalm 5:3

DAILY BIBLE VERSE

ADORATION

CONFESSION

THANKSGIVING

SUPPLICATION

DAILY PRAYER JOURNAL

By day the Lord commands his steadfast love, and at night his song is with me, a prayer to the God of my life. ~ Psalm 42:8

DAILY BIBLE VERSE

ADORATION

CONFESSION

THANKSGIVING

SUPPLICATION

Date

DAILY PRAYER JOURNAL

Out of my distress I called on the Lord; the Lord answered me and set me free.
~ Psalm 118:5

DAILY BIBLE VERSE

ADORATION

CONFESSION

THANKSGIVING

SUPPLICATION

If you then, who are evil, know how to give good gifts to your children, how much more will the heavenly Father give the Holy Spirit to those who ask him! ~ Luke 11:13

DAILY BIBLE VERSE

ADORATION

CONFESSION

THANKSGIVING

SUPPLICATION

Date

DAILY PRAYER JOURNAL

DAILY BIBLE VERSE

Let the words of my mouth and the meditation of my heart
be acceptable in your sight, O Lord, my rock and my redeemer. ~ Psalm 19:14

ADORATION

CONFESSION

THANKSGIVING

SUPPLICATION

Watch and pray that you may not enter into temptation. The spirit indeed is willing, but the flesh is weak. ~ Matthew 26:41

DAILY BIBLE VERSE

ADORATION

CONFESSION

THANKSGIVING

SUPPLICATION

But I say to you, Love your enemies and pray for those who persecute you.
~ Matthew 5:44

DAILY BIBLE VERSE

ADORATION

CONFESSION

THANKSGIVING

SUPPLICATION

DAILY PRAYER JOURNAL

For the eyes of the Lord are on the righteous, and his ears are open to their prayer. But the face of the Lord is against those who do evil. ~ 1 Peter 3:12

DAILY BIBLE VERSE

ADORATION

CONFESSION

THANKSGIVING

SUPPLICATION

Date

And whenever you stand praying, forgive, if you have anything against anyone, so that your Father also who is in heaven may forgive you your trespasses. ~ Mark 11:25

DAILY PRAYER JOURNAL

DAILY BIBLE VERSE

ADORATION

CONFESSION

THANKSGIVING

SUPPLICATION

And the Lord restored the fortunes of Job, when he had prayed for his friends. And the Lord gave Job twice as much as he had before. ~ Job 42:10

DAILY BIBLE VERSE

ADORATION

CONFESSION

THANKSGIVING

SUPPLICATION

DAILY PRAYER JOURNAL

Let everything that has breath praise the Lord!
Praise the Lord! ~ Psalm 150:6

DAILY BIBLE VERSE

ADORATION

CONFESSION

THANKSGIVING

SUPPLICATION

Bless the Lord, O my soul, and all that is within me, bless his holy name!
~ Psalm 103:1

DAILY BIBLE VERSE

ADORATION

CONFESSION

THANKSGIVING

SUPPLICATION

DAILY PRAYER JOURNAL

I will give thanks to the Lord with my whole heart;
I will recount all of your wonderful deeds. ~ Psalm 9:1

DAILY BIBLE VERSE

ADORATION

CONFESSION

THANKSGIVING

SUPPLICATION

My mouth is filled with your praise, and with your glory all the day. ~ Psalm 71:8

DAILY BIBLE VERSE

ADORATION

CONFESSION

THANKSGIVING

SUPPLICATION

Date

In God, whose word I praise, in God I trust; I shall not be afraid.
What can flesh do to me? ~ Psalm 56:4

DAILY BIBLE VERSE

ADORATION

CONFESSION

THANKSGIVING

SUPPLICATION

DAILY PRAYER JOURNAL

The Lord is my strength and my shield; in him my heart trusts, and I am helped; my heart exults, and with my song I give thanks to him. ~ Psalm 28:7

DAILY BIBLE VERSE

ADORATION

CONFESSION

THANKSGIVING

SUPPLICATION

Date

I cried to him with my mouth, and high praise was on my tongue.
~ Psalm 66:17

DAILY BIBLE VERSE

ADORATION

CONFESSION

THANKSGIVING

SUPPLICATION

Because your steadfast love is better than life, my lips will praise you. So I will bless you as long as I live; in your name I will lift up my hands. ~ Psalm 63:3-4

DAILY BIBLE VERSE

ADORATION

CONFESSION

THANKSGIVING

SUPPLICATION

Great is the Lord, and greatly to be praised, and his greatness is unsearchable.
~ Psalm 145:3

DAILY BIBLE VERSE

ADORATION

CONFESSION

THANKSGIVING

SUPPLICATION

DAILY PRAYER JOURNAL

And you will say in that day: "Give thanks to the Lord, call upon his name, make known his deeds among the peoples, proclaim that his name is exalted." ~ Isaiah 12:4

DAILY BIBLE VERSE

ADORATION

CONFESSION

THANKSGIVING

SUPPLICATION

Date

And let the peace of Christ rule in your hearts, to which indeed you were called in one body. And be thankful. ~ Colossians 3:15

DAILY BIBLE VERSE

ADORATION

CONFESSION

THANKSGIVING

SUPPLICATION

You will be enriched in every way to be generous in every way, which through us will produce thanksgiving to God. ~ 2 Corinthians 9:11

DAILY BIBLE VERSE

ADORATION

CONFESSION

THANKSGIVING

SUPPLICATION

DAILY PRAYER JOURNAL

Date

"To him who sits on the throne and to the Lamb be blessing and honor and glory and might forever and ever!" ~ Revelation 5:13b

DAILY BIBLE VERSE

ADORATION

CONFESSION

THANKSGIVING

SUPPLICATION

O Lord, you are my God; I will exalt you; I will praise your name, for you have done wonderful things, plans formed of old, faithful and sure. ~ Isaiah 25:1

DAILY BIBLE VERSE

ADORATION

CONFESSION

THANKSGIVING

SUPPLICATION

Date

God is spirit, and those who worship him must worship in spirit and truth.
~ John 4:24

DAILY PRAYER JOURNAL

DAILY BIBLE VERSE

ADORATION

CONFESSION

THANKSGIVING

SUPPLICATION

O God, you are my God; earnestly I seek you; my soul thirsts for you; my flesh faints for you, as in a dry and weary land where there is no water. ~ Psalm 63:1

DAILY BIBLE VERSE

ADORATION

CONFESSION

THANKSGIVING

SUPPLICATION

Date

DAILY PRAYER JOURNAL

For from him and through him and to him are all things.
To him be glory forever. Amen. ~ Romans 11:36

DAILY BIBLE VERSE

ADORATION

CONFESSION

THANKSGIVING

SUPPLICATION

Then you will call upon me and come and pray to me, and I will hear you.
~ Jeremiah 29:12

DAILY BIBLE VERSE

ADORATION

CONFESSION

THANKSGIVING

SUPPLICATION

Date

I stretch out my hands to you; my soul thirsts for you like a parched land.
~ Psalm 143:6

DAILY BIBLE VERSE

ADORATION

CONFESSION

THANKSGIVING

SUPPLICATION

DAILY PRAYER JOURNAL

There is none holy like the Lord: for there is none besides you;
there is no rock like our God. ~ 1 Samuel 2:2

DAILY BIBLE VERSE

ADORATION

CONFESSION

THANKSGIVING

SUPPLICATION

Date

I say to the Lord, "You are my Lord; I have no good apart from you."
~ Psalm 16:2

DAILY PRAYER JOURNAL

DAILY BIBLE VERSE

ADORATION

CONFESSION

THANKSGIVING

SUPPLICATION

Date

Now to him who is able to do far more abundantly than all that we ask or think, according to the power at work within us, ~ Ephesians 3:20

DAILY BIBLE VERSE

ADORATION

CONFESSION

THANKSGIVING

SUPPLICATION

DAILY PRAYER JOURNAL

Date

Let me hear in the morning of your steadfast love, for in you I trust.
Make me know the way I should go, for to you I lift up my soul. ~ Psalm 143:8

DAILY PRAYER JOURNAL

DAILY BIBLE VERSE

ADORATION

CONFESSION

THANKSGIVING

SUPPLICATION

And above all these put on love, which binds everything together
in perfect harmony. ~ Colossians 3:14

DAILY BIBLE VERSE

ADORATION

CONFESSION

THANKSGIVING

SUPPLICATION

Date

Let not steadfast love and faithfulness forsake you; bind them around your neck; write them on the tablet of your heart. So you will find favor and good success in the sight of God and man. ~ Proverbs 3:3-4

DAILY BIBLE VERSE

ADORATION

CONFESSION

THANKSGIVING

SUPPLICATION

DAILY PRAYER JOURNAL

So we have come to know and to believe the love that God has for us. God is love, and whoever abides in love abides in God, and God abides in him. ~ 1 John 4:16

DAILY BIBLE VERSE

ADORATION

CONFESSION

THANKSGIVING

SUPPLICATION

Date

We love because he first loved us. ~ 1 John 4:19

DAILY PRAYER JOURNAL

DAILY BIBLE VERSE

ADORATION

CONFESSION

THANKSGIVING

SUPPLICATION

That according to the riches of his glory he may grant you to be strengthened with power through his Spirit in your inner being, so that Christ may dwell in your hearts through faith–that you, being rooted and grounded in love. ~ Ephesians 3:16-17

DAILY BIBLE VERSE

ADORATION

CONFESSION

THANKSGIVING

SUPPLICATION

Date

Let love be genuine. Abhor what is evil; hold fast to what is good.
~ Romans 12:9

DAILY BIBLE VERSE

ADORATION

CONFESSION

THANKSGIVING

SUPPLICATION

This is my commandment, that you love one another as I have loved you.
~ John 15:12

DAILY BIBLE VERSE

ADORATION

CONFESSION

THANKSGIVING

SUPPLICATION

Date

May the Lord direct your hearts to the love of God
and to the steadfastness of Christ. ~ 2 Thessalonians 3:5

DAILY BIBLE VERSE

ADORATION

CONFESSION

THANKSGIVING

SUPPLICATION

DAILY PRAYER JOURNAL

But, as it is written, "What no eye has seen, nor ear heard, nor the heart of man imagined, what God has prepared for those who love him" ~ 1 Corinthians 2:9

DAILY BIBLE VERSE

ADORATION

CONFESSION

THANKSGIVING

SUPPLICATION

NOTES

Date

NOTES

Date

NOTES

Date

NOTES

Date

NOTES

Date

NOTES

NOTES

Date

NOTES

Date

NOTES

Date

NOTES

SEASONS

FALL PRAYER JOURNAL

Made in the USA
Lexington, KY
03 September 2019